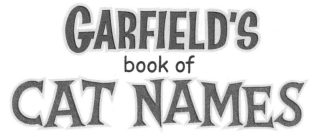

# GARFIELD'S
## book of
# CAT NAMES

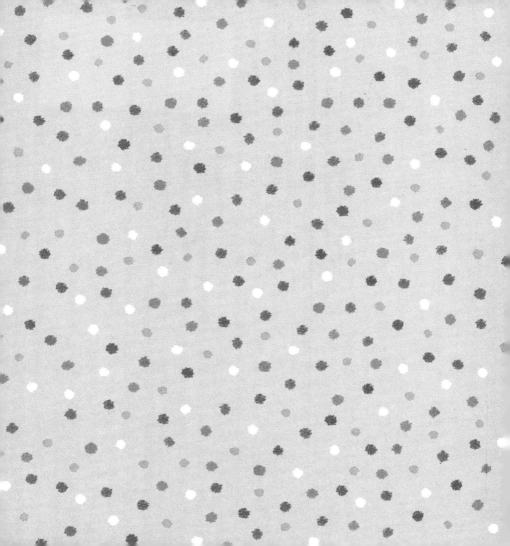

# book of CAT NAMES

"GARFIELD" IS MY NAME, BUT I'D PREFER "YOUR MAJESTY"

## BY JIM DAVIS

with Carol McD. Wallace and Mark Acey
Designed by Betsy Knotts

A Ballantine Books Trade Paperback Original

Copyright © 1988, 2005 by PAWS, Inc. All rights reserved.
"GARFIELD" and the GARFIELD characters are trademarks of PAWS, Inc.

Published in the United States by Ballantine Books, an imprint of The Random House
Publishing Group, a division of Random House, Inc., New York. This is a completely
revised edition of a work published by Ballantine Books in 1988.

BALLANTINE and colophon are registered trademarks of Random House, Inc.

Library of Congress Control Number: 2005908050

ISBN 0-345-48516-5

Printed in the United States of America

www.ballantinebooks.com

9 8 7 6 5 4 3 2 1

**Editorial**
Carol McD. Wallace and Mark Acey

**Design**
Betsy Knotts

**Illustration**
Lori Barker, Larry Fentz, Mike Fentz,
Brett Koth, and Lynette Nuding

**Production**
Linda Duell and Kenny Goetzinger

# CONTENTS

Some cats go through life as "Kitty." Some clueless owners don't see anything wrong with this. But robbing a feline of its individuality, denying it a decent name of its own – that's just wrong. Naming a cat is part of an owner's responsibility, like providing a lifetime supply of lasagna and kitty litter. A name a cat can sport with pride is just as important as love and shelter (though, admittedly, not as important as the lasagna).

Here are some other reasons to give your cat a name:

- So you can call it, and it won't come.

- So you can scream at it when it's shredded your drapes.

- So you can will it all your worldly possessions.

## Picking the Right Name

The wrong name can spell disaster. What cat named "Twinkie" ever got picked first for touch football? Was any president of the Rotary Club ever named "Fluffy"? Exactly. An appropriate name should allow plenty of room for growth, like an extra-large sweat suit. My own name recalls one of our country's finest presidents and has never given me a moment's embarrassment.

## Directions for Naming Your Cat

Remember that it won't be a namby-pamby kitten forever.

1. Make sure you know what sex it is. Consider John Wayne's embarrassment at being called "Marion" until they discovered he was "John."

2. Try calling the name out loud. Wouldn't you feel silly screaming "Tulip!" at the top of your lungs?

3. Don't listen to anybody else's advice except mine. They aren't cats.

## Using This Book

Given that most people have the attention span of a gnat, I've kept the book simple (like Odie) and filled it with lots of pictures (mostly of me, of course). The lists are alphabetical and shorter than "Mini Me" (now there's an inspired moniker). If you already know that you want to name your cat after a food (a sound choice), then you can turn directly to that section. Some of the names have a history you might want to know about – like "Attila the Hun." Some names mean things. "Hugh," for example, means "intelligence," an attribute of all felines. So I've tossed in some histories and meanings. They may be perfectly accurate . . . and then again, they may not be. We cats just live to toy with you humans!

# ATTRIBUTE NAMES

Sometimes people name their cats after a certain characteristic. Say it has white feet with lots of extra toes; you can call it "Bigfoot." If you got saddled with a Persian, you might call it "Puff" for its long hair; but don't expect me to be its friend.

On the other hand, people sometimes breed cats for perverse purposes. There is a new breed of cats with no hair. The kindly owner will tactfully rise above this characteristic and look for a name in another section of this book.

### ALBINIA
Latin for "white." Warning: white cats are expert shedders, especially on dark clothes just back from the cleaners.

### BLACKIE
You can do better than that, Bud.

### CLAW
A cat's best friend; a drape's worst nightmare.

### EGO
Great name for a narcissist. Some cats say "Meow"; yours says "Me first."

### FLABBY
Gives fat a bad rap. I prefer a positive spin such as "Flabulous."

### FLUFFY
Refers to an unmanageable coat. Cream rinse would take care of this unfortunate condition.

## JAWS
Affectionate tribute to the carnivorous nature of felines. Not recommended for lady cats, no matter how large their appetites.

## REX
Latin for "king." Good name for bossy type. Also, the name of a disadvantaged breed of cat that looks like a cross between an undernourished Siamese and a sheep.

## ROTUNDA
Latin for "round." Appropriate for plump female cats, but not very nice.

## SMOKE
What a gray cat looks like when he hears a can opener in a distant room.

## SOCKS
Unimaginative name given to cats with white paws. Yeah, I know there was a presidential puss with this

moniker, but the name's still lame. Besides, lapses in personal hygiene result in gray paws.

## SPEEDY
We cats, though often phlegmatic, are capable of quite a turn of speed. For instance, I've been clocked at 0 to 80 in five seconds when a hamburger was at stake.

## STRETCH
Refers to elasticity. Good name for a very limber cat – unless he objects to being named after a rubber chicken.

## WALLEYE
Well, there you are; not polite, but to the point.

## WINK
Cats don't, so forget about it.

## YAWN
Good for a laid-back cat. A yawn is as close as I come to exercise.

# DIMINUTIVES

"Diminutive," as those of us who write cat-name books know, means a short version of a name. It also means "little," so some of these names refer to size. Not all cats are lucky enough to grow as big as me. It seems cruel to stress nature's inequities, but if you insist, here's how.

**BABY**
Why would you want to name a cat after one of its natural predators?

**BETSY**
Short for "Elizabeth." Cuter but less regal than an English monarch. "Queen Betsy" could rule, say, a design studio.

**KEWPIE**
Name of ridiculously cute doll. Appropriate for female equivalent of Nermal.

**LILLY**
Short for "Lilliput," the island of really short people that Gulliver visited. Perfect for a teeny-weeny kitten.

**LITTLE JOHN**
Ironic nickname for Robin Hood's enormous friend. Cats don't appreciate irony; they think it's humans showing off.

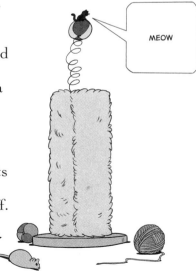

MEOW

**MIGNON**
French for "cute." Most
often used to describe a
steak, as in, "I would like
a cute steak for dinner."

**MINETTE**
French for "kitty." If
you aren't French, this
belongs in the "Preten-
tious" section.

**ODIE**
Short on brains . . . as in "not playing with a full deck."
Don't name a cat this unless it's beyond help, or you
hate it.

**PATTY**
Short for "Patricia." Also short for "mint patty,"
"hamburger patty," and "patty-cake."

**PEE WEE**
You wanna give your pet a complex? Remember, cat
shrinks are very expensive; the little couches are hard
to come by.

**PINKY**
Short for "pinkeye," perhaps?

**POOKY**
A confidant; someone with whom to share secrets. Not to be confused with "Porky," which is found in another animal-naming book.

**TABBY**
Short for "Tabitha," but, obviously, much cooler (and easier to spell).

**TEDDY**
Short for "Theodore," or "gift of God." Also short for "teddy bear," a cat's best friend.

**TINY**
You'll be the one feeling small if your itty-bitty kitty grows to a roly-poly furball.

# FOOD NAMES

Basically, people name babies and pets after what's important to them: beloved relatives, figures in history they admire, or maybe saints. What's important to me is food, and if more people were honest with themselves, they'd admit that it was important to them, too. You realize this when you see how many names you think are about something else, but actually refer to – guess what? – eating.

For my other big interest, see the section on sleep.

# FOOD NAMES

**BAGUETTE**
Très chic name for a puffed-up French poodle.

**CAL**
Short for "calorie," the best-tasting bits of any food. Take thousands; they're small.

**CARB**
Short for "carbohydrate," the stuff that makes life worth living.

**CAYENNE**
Your cat's destined to be hot stuff!

**CHOCOLATE**
A sweet, highly fattening substance; one of the four basic food groups.

**COCOA**
Warm drink made of milk and chocolate. Not to be confused with homonym "Coco," first name of famous and skinny French designer.

## EMERIL
The essence of a tasteful name. You could also kick it up a notch by nicknaming your cat "BAM"!

OH YEAH, BABE

## FEEDBAG
The snooty prefer to "dine"; the hearty like to strap on the feedbag!

## HOMINY
Southern corn dish of American Indian origin. AKA: Grits.

GARFIELD

## HOT DOG
Frankfurter. Also, derisive epithet for a show-off. As in, "Listen, Hot Dog, have you been climbing the drapes again?"

## JAM
Hip name for a happenin' cat. I jam; therefore, I am.

## MILKSHAKE

Combination of ice cream and milk popularly consumed as dessert, breakfast, or cocktail. Good name for a fluffy beige cat – or a pink one for that matter.

## MOUSSE

Could be one of three things: fancy name for pudding; large, not-too-bright antlered animal; or hair gunk, stuff no self-respecting cat would touch.

## NACHO

The Mexican answer to lasagna – *Olé!*

## PIZZA

A little slice of heaven.

## SANDWICH

In honor of English diplomat John Montagu, 4th Earl of Sandwich, who invented this breaded masterpiece in 1762. AKA: "Buns," "Sub," "Panini."

## SCAMPI

Primo name for an impish kitten with garlic breath.

# FOREIGN NAMES

I'm not much on traveling. If we were meant to go on trips, we'd have built-in odometers. Travel is supposed to broaden your mind, but my mind's the only narrow thing about me, and I like it that way.

Travel is fashionable though, and the farther you go, the better. (Going to the farm with Jon doesn't cut it.) Then you have to prove you've been there, with dopey souvenirs and boring snapshots, and keep reminding people. That's why you give a cat a foreign name.

# FOREIGN NAMES

### ASTRID
Teutonic for "impulsive in love." Swedish beauty with long blond hair who doesn't have the time of day for a mere cat.

### CARMEN
As in Carmen Miranda, famous Brazilian singer/dancer with hats made of unprocessed fruit salad.

### CASIMIR
Greeting from the mysterious East, home of turbans and pointy-toed slippers.

### GASTON
If you can live with a cat that eats snails and smokes strong cigarettes, be my guest.

### HANS
One of the ninety-seven forms of "John." Short for "Hansel." Everyone will ask where Gretel is.

### HEIDI
Either a "Swiss Miss" kitty who wears her ears in braids, or a leggy fine-feline supermodel type. You make the call.

### JACQUES
French for "James," not "Jack." (You can tell I've done my research.) But why not just call the cat "Jack" instead of having to correct everyone all the time?

### JUGNOO
Urdu/Hindi for "firefly." Good name for a bright cat with a taste for curried tuna.

### MARIO
"Warlike," in Italian. Between the naps and making all that lasagna, I wonder when they have time to fight.

### SOMBRERO
What you take a siesta under.

### SOPHIA
Means "wisdom." Sophia Loren's name. She's Italian. Probably makes great lasagna. Loves cats. Loves making lasagna for cats. Where's my passport?

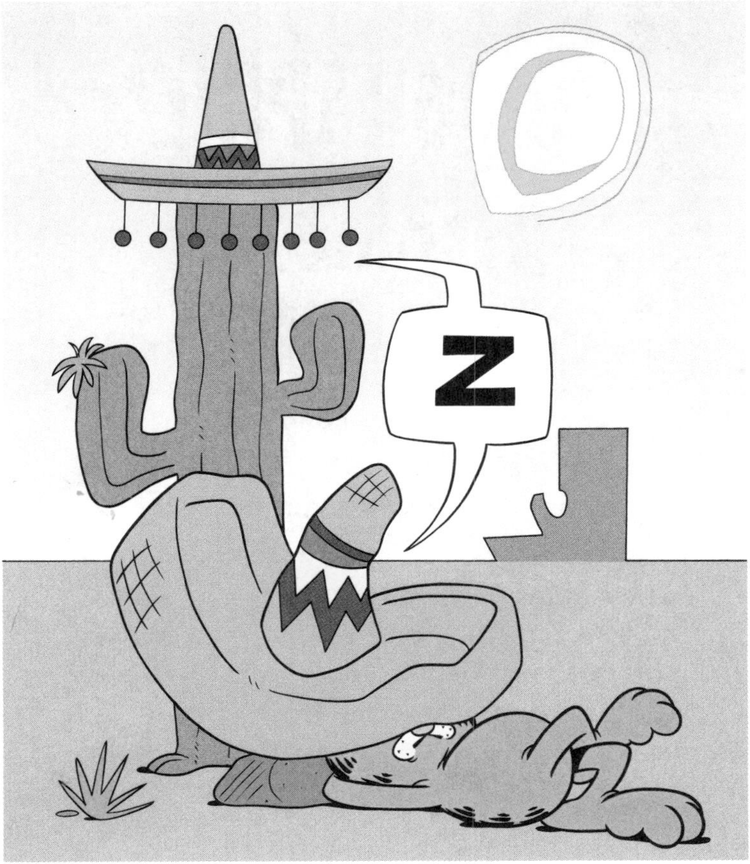
Z

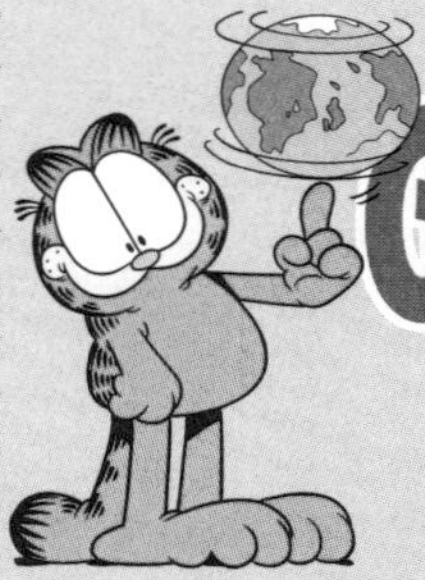

# GEOGRAPHIC NAMES

**Geography is about important places, like history is about important people. Places are important because important things happen there, like battles and the invention of different foods. Sometimes they are named after famous people, like Washington, D.C.**

**The names here reflect some key places, but you can think of your own. Like where you got your first speeding ticket. Where your grandparents came from. Where your favorite chocolate is made. Go on – name your cat "Hershey."**

### ABU DHABI
Capital of the United
Arab Emirates. I have a
warm spot for the name,
as I once mailed
Nermal there.

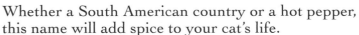

### BARCELONA
A gaudy cat with
miles of style and
flair to spare!

### CHILE
Whether a South American country or a hot pepper,
this name will add spice to your cat's life.

### CINCINNATI
Named after Cincinnatus, an ancient Roman states-
man. But the city's nickname, "Porkopolis," is nearer
and dearer to my stomach.

### EGYPT
Middle Eastern country where cats used to be
worshipped. Obviously, an advanced civilization.

### EVEREST

The highest mountain in the world, the ultimate challenge to mountain climbers. Maybe a name for the ultimate challenge to live with. I'm not talking about me; I'm talking about *Odie*.

### HAMBURGER

German adjective meaning "from Hamburg," the town that gave us one of my favorite foods. I thank them from the bottom of my stomach.

### KIEV

Russian city where butter squirts out of all the food.

HOP IN!

### MANHATTAN

A kind of clam chowder, inferior to "New England."

### MISSISSIPPI

River that has deep, dark mud named after a kind of chocolate pie.

## PARIS

Think the city, not the heiress. Très cool name for a sleek, chic cat.

## PHILADELPHIA

The name, like its trademark cheesesteak, is a mouthful. Go with "Philly". . . and some shoofly pie for dessert.

## SMALLVILLE

Okay, so maybe it is a *fictional* town in Kansas where Clark Kent grew up. But it's still a super name for a cat!

## STRASBOURG

Town in France, where geese are force-fed, a concept I don't understand.

## VEGAS

American center for flashy personalities and mecca for showbiz types like myself. I can see it now, in six-foot-high neon lights on the strip: "GARFIELD SINGS!"

# Historical Names

I was going to fill this section with cats I admired in history, but the big hitters of the feline world seem to have kept their exploits to themselves. This is typical of feline discretion. It forces me to turn to overachievers among humans, who aren't nearly as modest. (You should hear Jon bragging about his golf game.)

Some in this bunch are downright blood-thirsty, but that's what I admire: folks who know what they want and get it.

### ANASTASIA
Supposed only survivor of Russian royal family; good name for a cat inclined to put on airs.

### ATTILA THE HUN
Warrior-king notorious for the utter destruction he and his horde of barbarians left behind. "Hun" definitely not short for "Honey." Good name for a cat with a savage streak.

### DARWIN
A natural selection if you believe in survival of the *fattest*.

### DAVY CROCKETT
Frontiersman and hunter, famous for hunting bears and taming wildcats. (No relation to me.) Best of all, he gave the world the coonskin cap.

### GENGHIS KHAN
"Perfect Warrior." He adopted the name once he decided what he wanted to be. It goes to show what you can accomplish when you set your mind to something.

## HENRY VIII

Sixteenth-century English monarch.
Nobody could dispose of a drum-
stick (or a wife) like His Royal
Roly-Polyness.

## JULIUS CAESAR

Roman general whose motto was
"I came, I saw, I conquered."
I feel like that after every meal.

## LOUIS

Any one of seventeen kings of France, several of
whom wore Dolly Parton hair and high heels.

## MARIE ANTOINETTE

French queen who had her head cut off for suggesting
a change in the French national diet.

## MERLIN

Famous magician. Brilliant at making things disap-
pear. I can do that. . . . He could also make things
change shape – I can do that, too. I guess this means
that the multitalented Garfield is also a magician.
Maybe that's how I'll get to Vegas!

### NAPOLÉON
Short Corsican general who conquered Europe and gave his name to a pastry.

### NIMROD
"The mighty hunter." My spiritual brother; never mind that all I ever hunt is hamburgers.

### ROBIN HOOD
I approve of hanging out in the forest to surprise people, but this technique needed refinement. It should have been: Take from the rich and give to the *cats*.

### VICTORIA
Queen of England, Empress of India, and quite a gal. Good name for a plump cat who stands on her dignity.

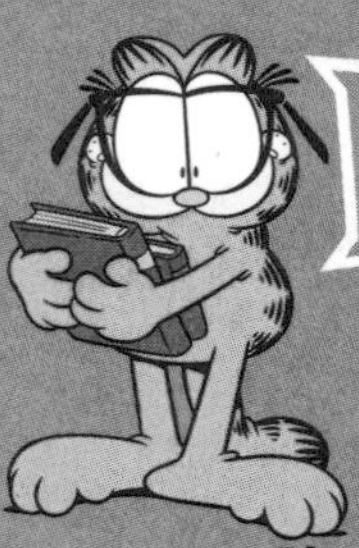

# LITERARY NAMES

**Since cats can't read, you might be wondering where I got these ideas. Culture, my friend, is in the air, free for all of us to breathe and absorb. Of course, cats have pretty small nostrils, so absorption is selective. I usually stick to the Classics Illustrated Comics.**

**AHAB**
Monomaniacal sea captain. Good name for a cat with a one-track mind.

**CATSBY**
Gatsby's a great name, but "Catsby" is even better.

**FALSTAFF**
Fat friend of the hero in Shakespeare's plays about Henry IV. No one ever talked about putting him on a diet. I was born too late.

**HAMLET**
I love any name with "ham" in it. To eat, or not to eat . . . that's a stupid question.

**HEATHCLIFF**
Whether your inspiration is *Wuthering Heights* or the comics, this obviously works for a cat.

**JEKYLL**
As in Dr. Jekyll and Mr. Hyde. Good for a cat with bipolar tendencies.

**JULIET**
Underage heroine of famous love story. Appropriate for cat who likes to moon around on balconies.

**KITTY**
Heroine of long, long, long book called *War and Peace*. Nobody will ever believe you read the whole thing. They'll also think you were just lazy and couldn't think up a better name for your cat. Then you will have wasted the price of this book.

**LINUS**
A towering figure in contemporary fiction. The other thing we have in common is we appreciate the value of a good blanket.

**MEDUSA**
Unpleasant character with snakes for hair. One look at her turned people to stone. That could be a pretty useful technique.

**MOBY**
Whale of a name for a fat cat . . . or a bald, bespectacled musician.

**MORGAN**
Witch in fairy tale who created castle made entirely of food. This is someone I'd like to meet.

**POLLYANNA**
Sappy heroine of children's story; perpetual optimist, in spite of all the evidence, including Monday mornings.

**QUASIMODO**
I have a hunch that this name will ring a bell.

**STEPPENWOLF**
Novel name for a cat (especially one who's born to be wild!).

**VOLDEMORT**
Appropriate choice if your little "Furry Potter" has crossed over to the dark side.

# MIGHTY MORONS

I considered putting Jon in this category, since as we all know he can be a real idiot, particularly where women are concerned. But I relented. After all, he's had the intelligence to stick with me.

It's not a big category, but I know it won't be a very popular one, either. After all, how dumb can a cat be?

**ALICE**
Silly blonde who fell down a rabbit hole and kept eating and drinking mysterious substances. Doesn't everyone's mother tell them not to take food from a stranger?

**BINKY**
Anyone who would rather throw a pie than eat it is a buffoon in my book.
Moronic moniker for a clownish cat, loud enough to annoy other galaxies!

**COLUMBUS**
What if the world had been flat? He would have sailed right off the edge. How smart is that?

**HANSEL & GRETEL**
Everybody knows that a trail of breadcrumbs scattered in the forest is going to get eaten. In a forest, even *I* would eat breadcrumbs.

**HEYWOOD**
Writer who started the rumor that all cats are gray in the dark.

# MORTAL ENEMIES

A cat doesn't get to my position in life without stepping on a few toes here and there. Sure, I try to be sensitive to the little guys, but, hey, you gotta do what you gotta do. I've been picked on, too, on the way up. So I'll admit it – I'm not a saint. I bear a grudge.

**BOBO**
A tough guy. Not a cat to meet in a dark alley.

**FIFI**
A French poodle – a freak of nature handicapped by a lousy haircut.

**JEAN**
First name of the founder of Weight Watchers. I'd like to make a dartboard out of her.

**LIBRA**
Latin for "scale." Get it?

**LIZ**
My vet. Jon's crush. She doesn't do either of us any favors.

**MR. POSTMAN**
In the natural order of things, mailmen are cats' traditional prey. It's just too bad so few cats know this. And so few postmen.

# MUSIC NAMES

You may think of me as a fat, lazy lug who only cares about food, sleep, and watching TV. But in my more animated moments I like to rock the house! Hey, I got the music in me – from classical to heavy metal and all that jazz in between. I'm the life of the party . . . and the party's not over till the fat cat sings!

### ALTO
Low female voice. Agitated Siamese.

### AMADEUS
AKA: "Wolfgang." A precocious cat who likes to run across the keyboard of your piano.

### ASHLEE
Sassy tabby synonymous with caterwauling and lip-syncing. AKA: "Milli Vanilli."

### BASS
Deep. As in the purring of a very happy, elderly tomcat.

### BEATLE
How to name one cat for the "Fab Four." Good choice for a long-hair.

### BOOTSY
Ahh . . . the name is funky, baby!
AKA: "Bootzilla."

### BOSS

A cat who was born in the U.S.A. . . . and born to run!

### CARUSO

Legendary tenor. I could give him a run for his money if I could only get a better agent.

### ELVIS

Old Norse meaning "all wise," though that doesn't explain the sequined bell-bottoms.

### FORTE

Loud enough to wake everyone in the house. VAR: Fortissimo, loud enough to wake everyone a block away.

### IDOL

As in American or Billy, depending on your generation. Good for a high-energy crooning cat. (Me, I'm more of an American *idle*.)

### LARGO
Tempo indication meaning "lethargic," though I prefer to think of it as "favoring economy of motion."

### MEATLOAF
Call him "Mr. Loaf" until you know him better.

### SHANIA
Pretty kitty with a torqued-up twang.

### SOPRANO
Highest voice – hungry kitten or very angry cat.

### STING
Grown man who used to prance around in yellow-and-black tights. Not a good role model for a cat.

**KSSSSHHH**

### STRAD
Short for Stradivarius, the famous violin maker. Do you know what violins used to be strung with?

### TENOR
High male voice; cats courting. That would be quite a high tenor.

### TINA
Diminutive of "Christine." Can you imagine how far "Ike and Christine" would have gotten?

### TRIANGLE
What the dummies in the marching band play.

### TUBA
Large brass instrument that makes noises like a giant digestive tract.

### USHER
Yeah, this is one cool (and hot!) cat.

### VIOLA
Stringed instrument whose case is just the right size for a catnap.

### ZEPPELIN
Blimp-size feline filled with a whole lotta love.

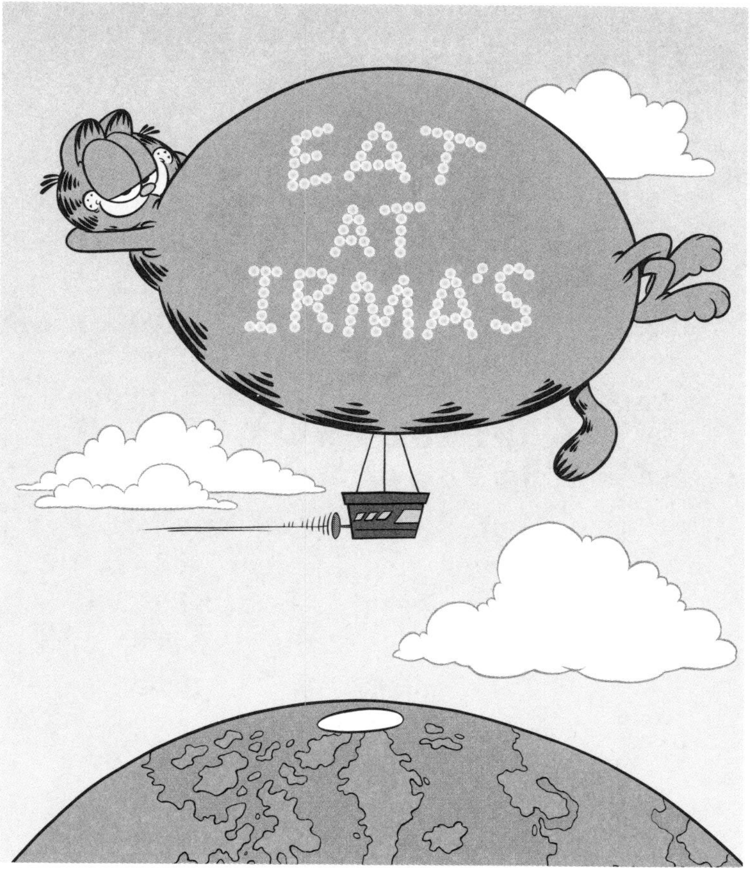
EAT
AT
IRMA'S

# NAMES TO AVOID

Some names get disqualified by association. You can't name your cat after the fat boy in third-grade homeroom, for instance. Or for the first person to stand you up for a date, or for an ax-murderer.

It's also important to respect the innate grace, wisdom, and dignity of felines. No cat ever comes when he's called, but believe me, he'll take to the streets if you name him something like "Lambykins."

## ARBUCKLE
From the Latin *arbuculus*, meaning "wiener-chested." A geek, a nerd, a geeky nerd; you get the picture. Your cat will be destined to be dateless.

## BELL
Device placed on cats by optimistic owners to trace their whereabouts. SYN: "Indignity."

## BRUTUS
Fancy name for "brute," e.g., any dog smarter than Odie and bigger than me.

## IRMA
The only person I've ever known who could put me off my food.

## LYLE
If it were a human, it would be an accountant. What options does that leave for a feline?

## MARTY
Short for "Martin." Evokes plaid suits, pinky rings, and toupees. More clash than class.

## MONDAY
Puh-leeze. I'd rather be named "Armpit."

## MULLET
Even if your cat is prone to bad fur days, this name is an achy-breaky-big-mistakey.

## POINDEXTER
Geekazoid who thinks reading the dictionary is the cat's meow. Good name for a nerdy kitty.

## SQUEAK
Hel-lo . . . it's a mouse name.

## TEMPERANCE
One of the seven cardinal virtues – used as a first name by the Puritans. I have no idea what it means.

## ZERO
Means "nothing" or "empty." As in, "this cat has zero personality" or "Jon has zero luck with women."

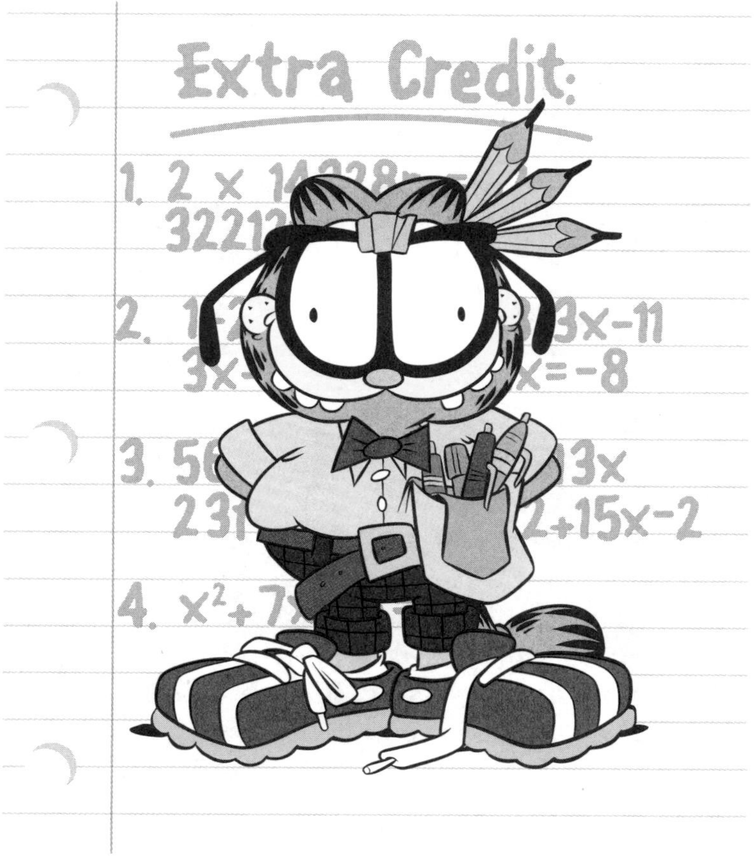
Extra Credit:

# NATURE NAMES

Jon is the real nature lover. Me, I love the great *indoors*. You can't take a TV on a camping trip because trees don't have electrical outlets. You can't order out for pizza. Besides, life in the wild can be dangerous. The leaves in the salad crisper don't give you diseases – but look at poison ivy. Normal house insects don't bite; they just compete with you for dinner – but look at red ants. Inside, mice are pests – outside, there are bears.
Don't step out the door:
**IT'S A JUNGLE OUT THERE!**

# NATURE NAMES

**BUNNY**
Another revoltingly cute animal, not very bright with sadly deformed ears. Don't name a cat after an animal so far below it on the phylogenetic scale.

**CLOUDY**
Weather condition in which my sunbeam is obscured. Also, what Odie's water bowl looks like when Jon forgets to change it for a week.

**DAISY**
Diminutive of "Margaret," don't ask me why. A sweet, old-fashioned kind of name, and a plant with great recreational potential.

**FAUNA**
Also, "Fawna," baby deer. Like "Bunny": nice house, nobody home.

**FERN**
A tender, yielding green plant; also, a terrific between-meal snack.

**HERBIE**
Short for "Herbert," meaning "glorious warrior." Jon
had a pet frog named Herbie once. I had a pair of frog
legs named Herbie shortly afterward.

**ICICLE**
For the coldhearted.

**IVY**
A clinging vine. Unlikely
to suit a cat, unless she's
very neurotic.

**PANSY**
Maybe an OK name for a flower,
but NOT your male cat!

**PEARL**
White beads made by oysters. My birthstone is the
only one that's also a food by-product.

**RANGER**
A cat's best friend in our national parks – he's the guy
who knows where the exit is.

## ROCKO
Also, "Rocco." Saint who cured Italians of the plague; also term for someone with minerals where the brains usually go.

## SASSAFRAS
A North American tree with aromatic leaves, or its dried root bark. I like the funny sound more than the funky scent.

## SKY
One of those hippie names like "Rainbow" or "Season"; for vege-tarians with macramé kitty beds and tie-dye blankies.

## STORM
This name's a natural for a tempestuous tabby with anger-management issues. Beware of battered-owner syndrome!

# OLD BUDDIES

Male bonding. Every fella needs some buddies to let his fur down with. No disrespect meant to the ladies, of course. But there are times in a cat's life when only the guy's guy will do. These are names for bachelors hanging out together; we all need moments like that.

## BUCKET

My best friend in kittenhood. He lived in a galvanized tin pan in a corner of a movie theater and gorged himself on buttered popcorn and jujubes. These days, I hear he's called "Angioplasty."

## CHEESER

AKA: "Cheeseball." Back in the day, we'd gourmandize and exercise. Now we just chew the fat and stretch the truth.

## CLARENCE

A good ol' cat from down home who spoke softly but carried a big baseball bat. Had a cute smile . . . especially after he took his teeth out before a fight.

## ED

Cat raised in a tree by squirrels. I couldn't persuade him to stay on the ground – he had a fear of low places.

### GUIDO
Italian form of "Guy" or "guide." Tough guy I met in my brief but colorful stay behind bars.

### GUS
Short for "Augustus," a real handicap in life. Can be overcome by a scrappy kind of cat with a quick left.

### HOWIE
Camp counselor who taught me all I know about the great outdoors – how to get back inside again!

### JIM BOB
Small-town cat who enjoyed big-time success. Has a solid-gold litter box and a refrigerator in every room.

### SPEEDO
Neighborhood tough who rode a skateboard. He met an untimely end on a supermarket loading dock, buried under a pyramid of canned creamed corn.

### SUSHI
Jon's goldfish. The only reason he's an old buddy is that Jon wouldn't let me turn him into a meal.

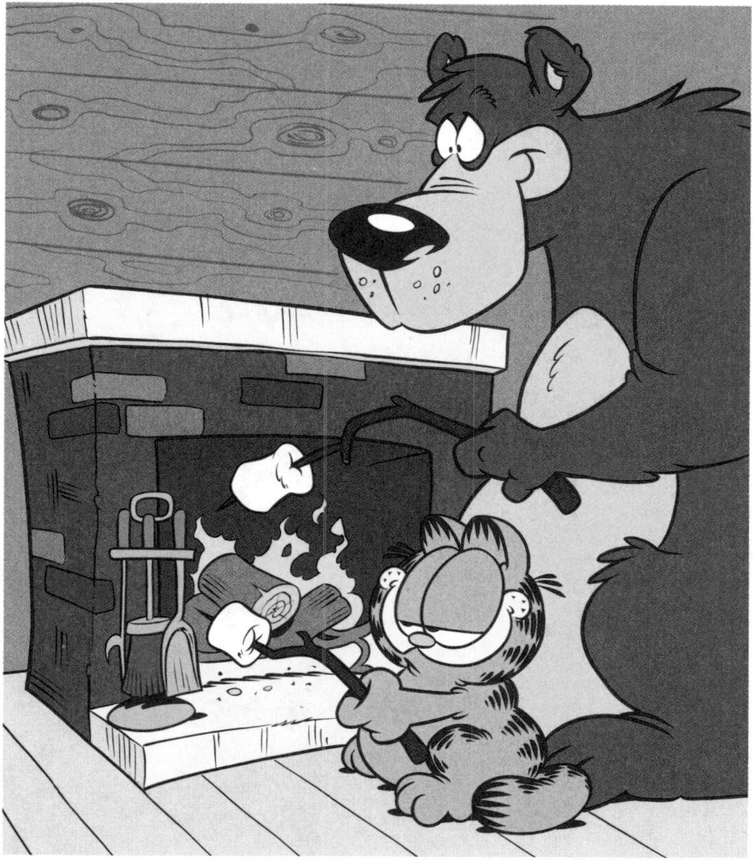

# OLD GIRLFRIENDS

Of course, a devastatingly attractive cat like me has quite a history with the females of the species. (Thankfully I've never had to undergo the humiliation Jon suffers; but then, look at Jon.) I wouldn't want to brag, but sometimes I wish I weren't quite so alluring to them. After all, I'll always be faithful to the love of my life – me.

## AMY

French for "close friend." We had a great time until she wanted me to leave my blanket at the house. I just wasn't ready for a commitment.

## ARLENE

My gap-toothed gal pal. She and I have a love-hate relationship: I love myself, and she hates that.

## BABE

Name to use in preliminary stages of relationship. As in, "Hey, babe, what's happening?," "Hey, babe, wanna have dinner with me?," or "Oh, babe, you have the most beautiful whiskers."

## BIJOU

She was a gem, all right, if you like the high heels and lots of jewelry type. Personally, I think they look stupid on a cat.

### BREE, EDIE, GABRIELLE, LYNETTE, and SUSAN

Five babes from the 'burbs who were frisky for me. Good names for desperate housecats.

### CRISPINA

Latin, feminine form of Crispin, meaning "curly haired." Sounds like a breakfast cereal to me.

### FATIMA

The only Siamese I've ever dated. Blue eyes to die for, but a voice like claws on a blackboard.

### GINGER

You don't have to be a professor to know this red-furred feline is a hottie.

### JASMINE

A sweet-smelling Persian and budding beauty. I bought her flowers but ended up eating them.

## PENELOPE

Greek name meaning "seamstress." She was just "sew-sew." Actually, she was sweet. We did a little TV work together – 'til I canceled her. Hey, that's showbiz.

## PRISCILLA

Latin for "of ancient lineage." There was nothing prissy about the one I knew; she drank out of Odie's water bowl on our first – and last – date.

## SYBIL

I liked most of her multiple personalities, but none of them liked me.

## TAMMY

VAR: Tammie, Tami, Tamee (tackee). Nice chassis, nothing under the hood. Perfect for the drum majorette kind of cat.

## ZOE

Greek for "life." I only took her out so I could say I'd dated cats from "A to Z."

# PEOPLE'S NAMES FOR CATS

It's considered a compliment to name a baby for a family member or friend. Obviously, it's even more of a compliment to give a person's name to a cat, who is sure to do it justice.

You can name a cat after your best friend, or your sister, or your boss, who's sure to be flattered. Or pick one of these names, including nicknames and their derivations, carefully selected for you by the world's expert on cat names – yours truly.

### ANGELA

DIM: Angie. Good name for slightly daffy blond kitten.

### ARNOLD

If a bodybuilder can become a governor, and a pig can become a TV star, then, obviously, this name's got major mojo.

### BETTY

Short for "apple brown betty," or "dessert with Garfield's name on it."

### CHIP

Short for "chocolate chip" or "potato chip" if you're a foodie. Short for "computer chip" if you're geeky.

### CHUCK

Short for "ground chuck," naturally.

### DOC

Jon's brother, also known as "Doc Boy." Believe it or not, Jon got all the looks in the family.

### ELLY MAY

If'n your hillbilly kitty likes
to hang out by the "ce-ment" pond,
this here name's for you.

### JOE

American slang for coffee,
the elixir of life. Nice name
if your cat's a java junkie
like me.

### JON

World's most common
name. There are 93 dif-
ferent forms of it in 27
languages. I'm afraid
my Jon is just as undis-
tinguished as his name.

### MARY

Most common female name. From Hebrew for
"bitterness." VAR: Maria, Marie, Maura, Marilyn,
Mamie, Muriel, Marilla, Mariquita, etc., etc. Unimaginative for a person; kind of cool for a cat.

**PHIL**

Short for "fill Garfield up."

**ROY**

From the French "roi," or "king." A name that
evokes mystery and power, as in "Evil Roy Gato"
and "Roy Rogers."

**RUBY**

Red precious stone. Generally an older woman who
calls you "hon."

**SPENCER**

As in the Spencer
Davis Group. Hip cat
with discriminating
taste in tunes. Classic
rock, sporty cars.

**VICTOR**

Stuffy name for "the guy who won."

# PRESIDENTIAL NAMES

There's no greater honor in the world than being president of the United States of America. And there's no greater honor for a cat than having a president's name. These aren't names for silly kittens like Nermal. These names have resonance. They're history. They're statesmanship. They're greatness.

## CARTER
Peaceful, peanut-loving puss.

## CLINTON
Slick name for a charismatic tomcat.

## COOLIDGE
President known for
his taciturnity, a quality shared
by most cats.

## FORD
Cornerstone of the great American tradition of football-
playing presidents.

## GARFIELD
As good as it gets. 'Nuff said.

## HAYES
Was given first Siamese in America, and liked it.
A seriously misguided man.

## KENNEDY
Ask not what your cat can do for you – ask what you
can do for your cat. AKA: "JFKat."

## LINCOLN
This is a perfect presidential name. Honest.

## MADISON
Husband of Dolley Madison, who was the first lady to serve ice cream in the White House.

## NIXON
Are you resigned to the fact that there's a bit of crook in your cat? AKA: "Watergate."

## POLK
Umm. Short for polka dot?

## REAGAN
A cat with hair to dye for and a penchant for jelly beans.

## TAFT
A man of majestic proportions, not unlike myself.

## TYLER
The president everybody forgets about when they're trying to list all the presidents. (He was tenth.)

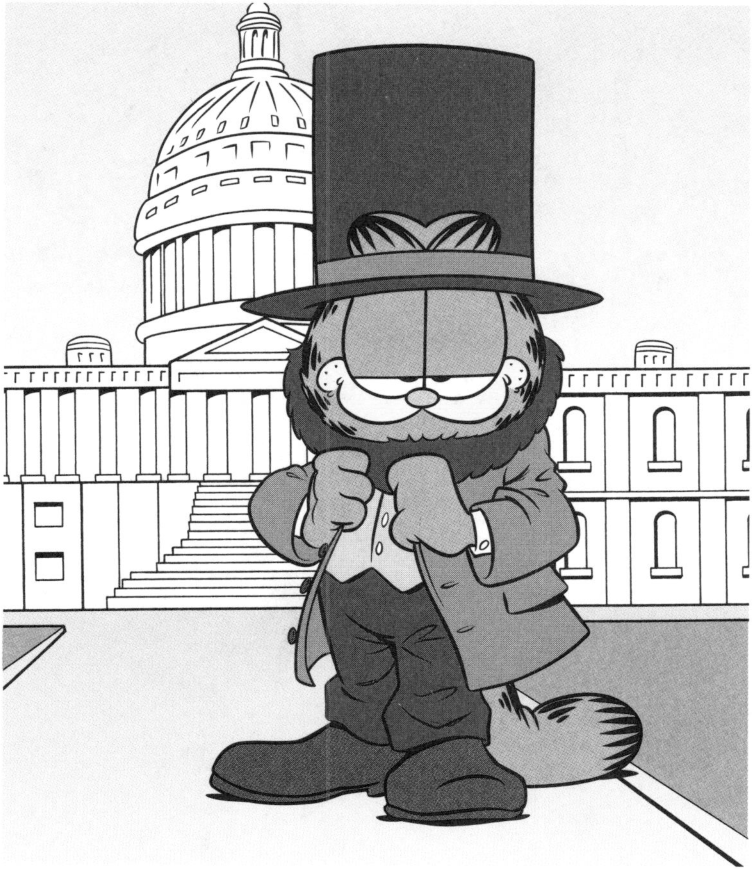

# PRETENTIOUS NAMES

Some humans think of a pet as an extension of themselves. It's true that dogs and their owners look alike, but cats aren't that easily influenced. If you want a cat as decoration, it might cooperate. Or it might be like me: decorative, I'm not. But I do make Jon a lot more interesting. How many people do you think would read a cartoon strip about *him*?

People who think of pets as accessories give them show-off names, but this pseudo-sophistication can't fool *moi*.

## ARISTOTLE
The name's Greek to me, as is his abstruse (another pretentious word) philosophy. Ditto for his teacher, Plato, and *his* teacher, Socrates.

## BÉBÉ
French for "baby." If that's what you want to name a pet, buy a tiny dog.

## COLETTE
French writer who was very fond of cats but isn't that famous. Real graduate-student kind of name.

## HARLEQUIN
Fancy clown, dressed in black and white. Cats never clown without very good reason – like lasagna.

## MAGNUM
If you have a TV show in mind, you're a real person. If you plan to name your pet after a big bottle of champagne, I'm not so sure.

### MAX
Short for Maximilian, maybe? Maxwell? Maximum?
Maximum snob appeal, if you ask me.

### NUREYEV
Great Russian ballet dancer, famous for his leaps.
Good name if you can't think of anything else, since
every cat prides itself on its grace.

### ODYSSEUS
Ancient Greek who got lost on his way home from a
war. Admirable name for a tomcat with an adventur-
ous nature.

### PICASSO
Ultrafamous Spanish
painter. Not very con-
vincing if you want to
show off your culture
since everybody in the
world has heard of him.

### PRINCIPESSA
That's "princess" to the
hoi polloi.

## RODIN
Influential nineteenth-century French sculptor. Perfect if your cat is a big thinker.

## THOREAU
If you want to simplify, as this American philosopher suggests we do, you can start by giving your cat a normal name. So forget "Walden," and go with "Wally."

## VITRUVIUS
Ancient Roman architect. Show-off name because nobody knows who he is except real know-it-alls like *moi*.

## YALE
Sounds Ivy League smart, *n'est-ce pas*? But before your cat's head gets too big for his mortarboard, keep in mind that this English word means "mountain goat."

# SIDEKICKS

The Caped Avenger leads a swashbuckling existence, but his life was slightly empty (but a lot less annoying) until he met his trusty sidekick Slurp.

The sidekick's role is to be supportive, smooth the way for the hero, and ask dumb questions to make the hero feel smarter – not unlike the owner-pet relationship. In fact, if you're really honest, you might want to think about who's the sidekick: you or your cat?

## BARNEY
As in classic '60s sidekicks Barney Fife and Barney Rubble. Unfortunately, the name has since been sullied by an insipid dinosaur. Now best to avoid unless your cat is purple.

## CUPID
The little guy who does all the dirty work for Venus, goddess of love.

## KATO
Served as chauffeur and assistant to "The Green Hornet." But this kung-fu fighter knew that anytime he wanted, he could pull the car over and kick his boss's butt.

## OLSEN
Think Jimmy, not the twins. Dorky cub reporter in bow tie who gets in trouble so Superman can rescue him.

## ROBIN
The only one who really knows how to operate all the optional features on the Batmobile.

### SAM
Short for "Samwise," Frodo's sidekick. Good for a cat who's a brave and loyal companion . . . and, of course, a creature of "hobbit."

### SANCHO PANZA
"Panza" is Spanish for "pot belly." He was the brains behind Don Quixote.

### TONTO
Faithful Indian companion to "The Lone Ranger." His name means "fool" in Spanish; however, he was the one smart enough to be bilingual. And he didn't have to wear that silly mask, either.

### V.P.
Short for "vice president," the quintessential sidekick.

### WATSON
Victim of Sherlock Holmes's condescension. He couldn't be as dumb as he pretended if he wrote down all those stories.

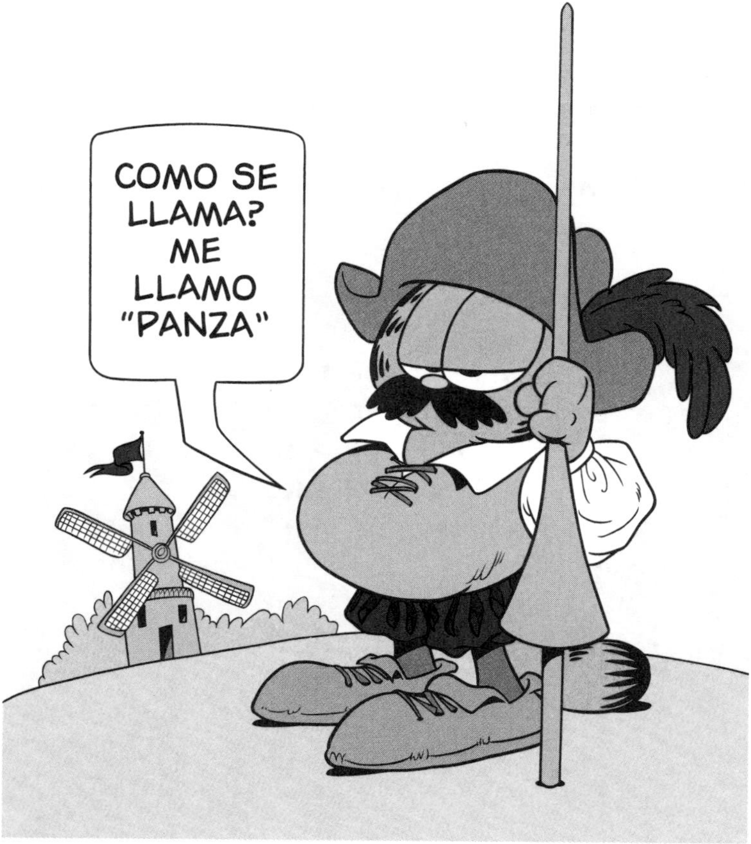
COMO SE LLAMA? ME LLAMO "PANZA"

# SLEEP NAMES

There are two ideas about sleep. Some people say, "You can sleep when you're dead" and boast about sleeping only four hours a night. The other attitude is, "It's a third of your life, so you might as well enjoy it." You can guess which way I feel. Fortunately, I'm not one of those types who needs elaborate props to sleep. No, sir: no silk sheets, earplugs, hot toddies for this cat! I just respond to the call of nature. . . .

## HIBERNATION

Sleeping all winter. Even I think this is taking things a little too far.

## LULLABY

Song you sing to make a baby sleep.

## MR. SANDMAN

The guy who sprinkles sand in your eyes to make you sleep. I personally have never had to resort to this technique.

## NARCOLEPSY

Fancy word for nap attacks.

## NOD

As in "to nod off to sleep."

## RIP

Short for Rip van Winkle, henpecked husband who went drinking with dwarfs and passed out for twenty years. Suitable for cat who likes marathon naps.

### SIESTA

Naptime in foreign countries where it gets hot during the day, and they eat dinner after my bedtime.

### SLEEPING BEAUTY

A pretty light sleeper if a kiss was enough to wake her up!

### SLOTH

Lazy, slow-moving mammal that lives in South American trees. Also, what I feel like on Monday morning.

### SNOOZE

Affectionate nickname for the main activity.
VAR: Slumber, Doze.

### SOMNAMBULA

Fancy name for a woman who walks in her sleep. I occasionally do this and miraculously find myself in front of the refrigerator. Then, for a real peak experience, I eat in my sleep.

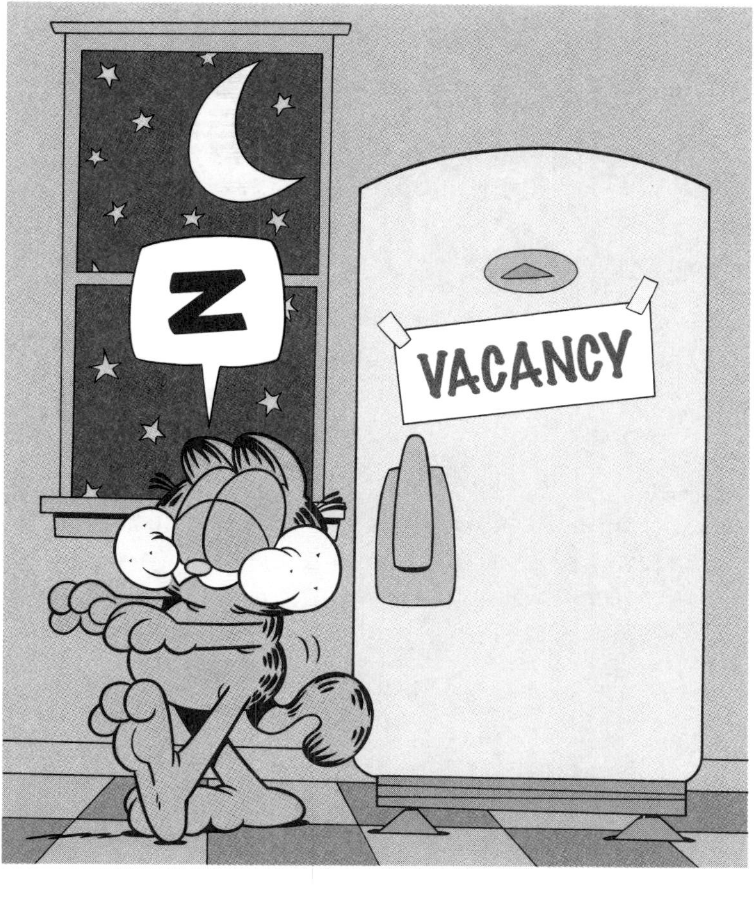
Z
VACANCY

# SPIRITUAL NAMES

Cats have always had an air of the otherworldly – in fact, the ancient Egyptians had the good taste to worship us for around 2,000 years. Talk about "good old days"!

Names dealing with the spiritual realm are simply divine. And if you've been nice to your cat, it might put in a good word for you with the Big Guy Upstairs.

### ADAM
The first man; the first litter-box changer.

### ATHENA
Greek goddess of war who sprang fully armed from her father Zeus's head. Forerunner of the migraine.

### BASTET
Egyptian cat goddess whose specialty was fertility. Worship included annual orgies of food and drink and . . . food and drink.

### BUDDHA
Large guy with a protruding belly and a calm disposition. Big on staring into space. Venerated by millions in the East. I want his job when he retires.

### GABRIEL
Angel who brings news. Appropriate for the one cat in a million who will carry a newspaper in its mouth.

### JEROME
Saint who translated the Bible into Latin and kept a cat to whom, scholars say, he fed a lot of lasagna.

### MOSES
Baby found in a basket. Good name for foundling cat, except the basket always holds three or more kittens.

### NOAH
Lifeguard to the animal kingdom. Showed very poor judgment issuing boarding passes to dogs, spiders, and mailmen.

### SALOME
First recorded "exotic dancer"; the Rockettes owe everything to her.

### SAMSON
Strong man in the Bible, until he got a haircut. Good name for a Maine coon cat.

### THANKSGIVING
Act of giving thanks for the good things in life. Also, one of Garfield's favorite holidays – and, believe me, not because of football.

### VISHNU
Hindu supreme spirit, with four arms (also two legs). I could accomplish a lot with two extra arms.

### YVES
Patron saint of lawyers, often represented by a cat, which is like a lawyer in terms of intelligence, stealth, strategic abilities, discretion, and standing in the community.

# SPORTS NAMES

Cats generally have more sense than to run around working up a sweat in the name of fun. To me, chewing and sleeping are the perfect exercises. And cross-training is eating in bed.

However, cats are gifted athletes and can run circles around dogs (except we're too smart to run around in circles). Even I once punted Odie more than 50 yards! So, if you're a sports fan, you might want to pick a name for a cat who's got game.

## BABE
Works for both males and females, as in baseball legend Babe Ruth or track, golf, and all-around athletic great Babe Didrikson. Good name for cats who can hit the long ball (chicks dig that!).

## GRETZKY
Great name for a cat who plays "mice hockey."

## LeBRON
This cool cat shoots hairballs and can jump out of the gym!

## MIA
You'll get a kick out of this name if your cat's a little ham.

## TIGER
If your cat loves to play around in the woods, this name will suit him to a tee.

# TURNABOUT: CAT NAMES FOR PEOPLE

Earlier, I covered some people's names for cats. So, I figured I'd do the ol' switcheroo and offer a few feline names for people. It's considered an honor to name a baby after a relative or friend. So why not name a baby for a cherished cat? Here are some traditional cat names for parents without beloved cats of their own. If you already have a cat, then just use its name. The baby is sure to be the only "Felix" in its kindergarten class.

### CAT
Even a completely unimaginative cat owner with a taste for the obvious can find something better for his pet. For a human, though, it has a certain raffish charm.

### GARFIELD
I mentioned this earlier, but some things bear repeating. Name of one of the world's most charismatic cats – an inordinately handsome, witty kitty, possessing enormous intelligence (and an even greater appetite). Any human should be honored by this name. Hey, it was good enough for a president of the United States!

### KIT
As in Kit Carson, the famous frontier scout. Or, for you boob-tube buffs, the talking car in "Knight Rider."

### KITTY
Hel-lo . . . this name is perfect for a cute little girl.

# UNISEX NAMES

English unisex names are nothing new: They've been around since the Middle Ages. But they've become trendier in recent times. Whether these gender-neutral names sound classy or bratty is up for debate. But they *would* seem to cause confusion: It's hard sometimes to tell little girls and boys apart.

Still, there may be people who don't have access to a vet, and can't tell what kind of cat they have. I offer these names as a service to spare the world cats named "Thomasina" and "Bobette."

### ANGEL
Let's face it: Most cats are not angels. Better name for a vampire.

### ASHLEY
Wimpy character in *Gone With the Wind* with whom Scarlett O'Hara falls in love – even though Rhett Butler could eat him for breakfast.

### HILARY
VAR: Hillary. From Latin meaning "cheerful." As in "hilarious." For the unusual cat who's easily amused. Or a cat with presidential aspirations.

### JORDAN
Hebrew name meaning "descend." People used to think of the famous River Jordan; now they think of the famous player Jordan.

### RANDY
Good name for a frisky cat, if you know what I mean!

# WACKY & WEIRD NAMES

Last, but not in the least normal, are names that are crazy. That is, unless your cat is rich, then the names are merely eccentric. These range from simply silly to knick knack patty wack, outrageously out there. Choosing a name for your cat isn't science, but it can be weird. Choose one for your quirky kitty.

### BATES
As in Norman Bates. Perfect if your cat's a psycho.

### BLING BLING
Diamonds are a cat's best friend.

### BOY GORGE
Nutty name for a cross-dressing
fat cat.

### BURPO
Name of the Marx Brothers'
cat. Well, if it wasn't, it should
have been.

### GHERKIN
Weird, but it still beats being
called "Pickles."

### JENIUS
Ironic name for a moronic cat.

### LIPO
As in "liposuction." For a cat who is destined for an
extreme makeover.

Now you know which names are good for cats, and which names will cause them to use your shoes as a litter box. If none of these seem appropriate, better double-check the cat: You may actually be trying to name a shrub or a toaster by mistake. And, obviously, this list is not exhaustive (though I'm exhausted and could use a nap).

Of course, as a last resort, you could always name your cat "Anonymous," in which case your cat will surely think of a few choice names to call *you*! In the final analysis, however, it doesn't really matter what you name your cat, because cats don't care what you call them, just as long as you call them for dinner.